BEGIN WITH YES

21 Day Companion Workbook

A step-by-step guide to living your Begin With Yes life

Except when an individual's complete name is used, people mentioned in this book are fictitious composite characters intended to illustrate specific issues and situations.

Toby Dog Publishing
ISBN-13: 978-0692465837
ISBN-10: 0692465839

Cover photographs by Michael Wynne
www.michaelanthonywynne.com

TABLE OF CONTENTS

ACKNOWLEDGEMENTS

It seems fitting that these words of acknowledgement would take shape as I visit the ocean. I grew up here and often return to regain a sense of connectedness, peace and calm. As I sit here, holding the last draft of the manuscript I know this workbook would not have happened without the love, hard work and creative mind of my dear friend and editor for this project, Jacob Nordby. We seem so in synch with each other and with this book's principles that I often smile to discover I can't remember where my words end and Jacob's begin. It has been a beautiful and magical collaboration to be sure. Jacob is an author I met before he first published and it has been marvelous to watch him live out the Begin With Yes journey as he connected with his dreams and made them real.

Artist and writer Barb Black lent her superior skills as

grammarian and proofing editor to this project.

Author Craig Hart handled the manuscript design and ebook conversion.

I want to thank my children, including their spouses and my grandchildren—who love me despite my imperfections and continue to laugh at my jokes, allowing me to think I'm funnier than I really am. I bet I love you more than even I know and certainly much more than you can imagine.

This workbook grew out of my very first book "Begin with Yes", the subsequent growth I have had, and the countless like-minded, inquisitive and helpful teachers I have met along the way. You will get to know me better as you move through these twenty one days of exploring, but you will more often see yourself reflected in beautiful, hopeful and optimistic ways in the pages that follow. I want to acknowledge and thank each person who helps co-create our Facebook page. You continue to bless my days and my work, and you are the warm sun I feel on my face as I listen to the waves right now.

DEDICATION

For Mike who sees me through the loving, rose-colored glasses he chooses to wear. You are a beautiful, handsome gift that surprised me when I least expected it. I am grateful for all that we have shared and look forward to many more sunsets and sunrises as we discover what's around the next corner—and the one after that too...

INTRODUCTION

I wrote *Begin With Yes - A Short Conversation That Will Change Your Life Forever* and published it in 2009. I could not have known what an amazing journey would unfold from that first step. It's funny to say that, because first steps are exactly what the book is all about. If you have read the book already, you'll know that I wrote it after a period of intense change and unsettling, sometimes depressing events in my own life. My desire was to offer the discoveries I made during that time which changed my course and helped me access my own power to step into a new, more expansive way of living on every level.

The things that have happened since I held the first copy of the baby book in my hands fill me with amazement every day. I just couldn't know how powerful this simple message would be for so many people. I am humbled and grateful as I watch the Begin With Yes family grow from just a few to over a million from around the world.

After the book began to reach far beyond my personal sphere of friends and acquaintances, I began to receive many requests to help people install the Begin With Yes principles in their real lives. I realized that the time had come to design a practical tool which would allow me to offer my hand and help you step across the line into that first inspired action which changes everything.

That is when this workbook was conceived.

It is designed to be a companion for *Begin With Yes*, the book. I encourage you to read it first, then use this workbook as a way to see your own life through new eyes and create real magic for yourself and those around you. In some ways imagine me being with you as you move forward through this process.

From my years in the business world, I know that one of the hardest things to do after coming upon a great idea is to implement it. Many people read *Begin With Yes*, get inspired by the philosophy, and set about to change their lives. Because old habits have a way of dying hard, often they get tangled up in those patterns and find themselves right back in their old way of thinking and acting. My intention with this Workbook is to help you implement a new template for living your life. There is good science behind this because researchers have learned that to make meaningful change, we actually have to carve new neural pathways in the brain. That is what we will do together as you go through the exercises and take them out to walk in the real world. You are literally changing your mind!

This is a 21 Day Guide. I would love it if you could imagine that you and I are taking a little walk every day to talk about your life and find ways to apply the Begin With Yes principles in your world.

So, since every journey must begin somewhere, I think it is time we get started.

Are you ready to begin? Ah...good. I was pretty sure your answer would be yes.

INSTRUCTIONS

Writing — You will find some places along the way where I ask you to write a little. I chose not to fill this book with blank lines, so if you will purchase an inexpensive notebook and a pen that works, you will be well equipped to use the simple journaling exercises. You may have a larger budget or just want to buy a beautiful journal. That's fine, too. Just be sure that whatever you use is especially for this 21 Day transformation. You will want to look back to this time someday in the future and it will help if you know where to find your notes. Also, please be sure to keep your journal in a safe, private place. For this process to go deep, we need to be sure not to sugarcoat anything. You can share your discoveries later, but I encourage you to write this just for yourself at the moment.

This will be easy. I will ask you questions and you will write answers. You don't need to be a great writer, and I promise to give you prompts that will help get you started. In many cases, you may only need to write one or two word answers. Doesn't sound too daunting, does it?

Visualizations — In some places I will offer you visualizations to help activate your imagination and move you into a receptive state of mind. I invite you to read over the instructions a couple of times, then find a safe, quiet place to enter this zone. If you need to wait until you get home or some other place which will allow you to have a few peaceful moments, that's a good idea. None of these exercises will require more than a few minutes at a time, so don't worry that you are taking on a huge practice. My intention is to make this experience powerful, bite-sized, and deeply affirming for you—one day at a time.

Daily Steps — I have broken Begin With Yes into twenty-one short, daily steps. My intention is that the reading is easy and the exercises fit well into a busy lifestyle. If you miss a day, I encourage you to pick up again and continue without worrying about it. Also, although the exercises and lessons build on each other, so if you find yourself moving back and forth, that's okay, too. The main thing here is that I offer you my hand and help as you move your feet in the direction of your true desires. Each day begins and ends with a thought. Please take three to five minutes at the start and finish of the day and read those words. Let them sink in. Allow the questions to plant themselves like seeds in your consciousness and watch them sprout into new growth which will soon appear above the surface in your life—these things will bear fruit in surprising ways.

Day One

As the day unfolds, take a moment to remember the good things already in your life. Then with arms and heart open wide, gently move into your day.

As thoughts drift into your mind, carefully sort them. Those that are worthy and helpful, use to shape your actions. And those that are unworthy and hurtful, gently move aside and forget.

Hello!

I wish you could know how happy I am to see you here at the beginning of this twenty-one day Begin With Yes adventure.

Oh, by the way, that's how I see this, too.

It is an adventure into

- Who You Are
- What You Desire
- and How To Bring It Into Your Life

I wonder if you would pretend something with me for a few minutes?

Imagine that you and I just met for a walk along the beach. (I am actually editing this book right this minute at a beach near my house on one of the first warm days of Spring. My shoes are off and my toes are in the sand.) Here we are at the end of a long pier stretching out across the surf which washes the shore below us. Since we're just getting to know each other, I turn and ask you a question.

"Will you tell me about yourself?"

"You mean, what I do for a living?"

"No, if you don't mind, give me a short story of you.

Where were you born, what you've done—that sort of thing."

Imagine that you look far out to sea where the sun is just coming up, turning the water all pink and gold. Your mind travels back in time to your first memories...

BEGIN AT THE BEGINNING

Write Your One Page Biography

In your new notebook or journal, please write a brief summary of your life so far. Don't try to capture everything, but just begin writing and see where it takes you.

"I was born...

We'll continue this conversation tomorrow, but for today, I ask you to let yourself remember your own journey in life so far. As you go about your day, just open yourself to memories when they show up. Whether they are pleasant or full of pain, don't dwell on them—just let them play like movie clips you are watching.

Part of the *Begin With Yes* process is to remember and to get in touch with who we are. This helps us connect with our true desires and also the things which have hurt us, held us back in the past, or otherwise halted our progress.

Before You Go To Sleep...

Tonight be in touch with your innocence.
The deeper, more authentic you
where all the hurts and disappointments,
all the mistakes, regrets and wrong turns
are pushed aside and the real you once again emerges
into the warm light of acceptance, peace and love.

I'm going to remind you that this is meant to be a daily experience, so it would be a good idea to let everything from Day One settle in while you rest tonight and begin again tomorrow on Day Two.

Day Two

Sometimes, like a low grade fever,
we've lived with anxiety, fear, anger or resentment
for so long we've forgotten that this isn't how
we were meant to feel.
If this an issue with you, the first step is
to decide you don't want to feel like this any longer.
The second and more difficult step is
to ask, "What would I have to do to feel better?"
Your answer could be the beginning of
a whole new way of life!

Yesterday we took a little walk by the ocean and I asked you to tell me about yourself. I wonder what came up for you when you traveled backward in time through your own landscape of memories?

Did you feel the highs and lows? Did you notice any long-standing patterns?

I invite you to ponder the quote which begins this day for a few minutes. As you look back over your life, what are the things which stand out as your pains? Maybe a different word is "disappointments".

WHAT HURTS

Your Top Ten Disappointments

Please find a new page in your notebook and write ten things which represent real disappointments in your life. You may only need one or two words for each one, but it's okay if you find yourself writing more.

"This happened...

You might be wondering why we are starting here. Well, we'll get to the joyous things soon, but, the truth is, the reason most of us would even get into a book like *Begin*

With Yes is because we really need and want something to change. If everything was already smooth and happy, we wouldn't have much reason to go looking for answers, would we?

So, I ask you to list your disappointments because I want us to be completely honest with each other. Let's start with the "elephant in the room", shall we?

What I always find fascinating about this exercise when I'm working with someone is that these things are all connected. When we look deeply into your past disappointments or hurts, we will soon find patterns which may not be obvious at a first glance.

This can be the real beginning of transformation and healing.

Before You Go To Sleep...

Are you frustrated or angry with
someone who is trying to manage your life for you?
If so, I don't blame you--that's your job!
Sometimes a gentle reminder is all it takes.
Other times you need to come right out and
say it more forcefully.
Of course some people will be relieved,
and others will resist.
Either way your job is to focus on your own life
and keep moving forward.
Drift gently tonight.

In the still of the night you will often hear
the distant music of your heart.

I'm going to gently suggest that you stop reading now and
pick up tomorrow with fresh eyes and heart.

DAY THREE

Don't let feelings get in the way of actions.
"Begin with Yes" is not about
sticking your head in the sand and pretending that
everything is wonderful all the time.
But it is about taking a small
(sometimes very small)
step even when you're not feeling it!
And so we begin.

It's completely possible to be grounded in reality and
remain open to possibilities and magic, too.

Today we're sitting together in a coffee shop. People are coming and going, the sounds of busyness are around us everywhere, and espresso being steamed, and newspapers being rustled.

"So, how is it going for you right now?"

I ask you this question, then lean back and take a sip of coffee. I'm interested in what you are finding out about yourself, what you are noticing or discovering, and, even more important, how you are feeling as this process unfolds.

Go ahead and answer. Pretend you can let your eyes meet mine and just tell me anything that comes up. I can handle whatever you need to say. Sometimes people think that I'm all about positive attitude and they feel badly about being honest when things are bothering them. While I am the "Optimist In Chief" at Begin With Yes, I know that there isn't any way to release negative feelings without allowing them to surface. Otherwise they just stay stuck in there.

After you have allowed yourself to tell me whatever is on your heart and mind in this imaginary conversation (I hope you really will pretend that you are talking to me, you might be surprised at how real it feels), I'd like to shift our direction a bit.

I invite you to stay in imagination for just a little while. Here's my question:

If you had a fairy god mother or father
suddenly show up
and your life would magically change
because they had the power to do anything you need,
what would happen?

THE MAGIC WAND

Write for a few minutes about what would happen in your life if someone with magical powers could eliminate things, change things, and give you new possibilities.

"I would wish for...

I have a very specific reason for asking you to do this. It's called a "change of state". Psychologists and other researchers have discovered that when we are in a particular mental cycle, it is hard to see outside of it. A pattern-interrupt is required to open our minds to anything outside that feedback loop.

So pretending isn't just wishful thinking. It actually affects our neurochemistry and physiology. We can change the way we feel in our minds and bodies with simple things like this. When we do, we become more open and expansive rather than tight and contracted.

Can you feel the difference?

Today I invite you to play with the "magic wand" whenever you run into a painful thought or a hard situation. Just ask yourself what you would like to change about that. It isn't necessary to do anything yet. Just imagine what you would like to change.

Before You Go To Sleep...

Are you worried about tomorrow?
Or are you learning that
worry is the most over-rated,
unproductive pastime ever invented?
If there's some small step you can take tonight
that will improve the odds for tomorrow, take it.
And if not,
(or after that small step)
go for a walk or listen to some music,
call a friend, see a funny movie,
and go to sleep counting your blessings instead!

PAUL S. BOYNTON

Day Four

Lack of self-confidence and self-esteem
can slow us down or even keep us stuck,
but don't let that stop you from taking a step today.
Discover for yourself that
action actually builds our self-esteem
and as we move forward our confidence will grow.
One step today even if you don't yet believe!

As we meet today, I'd like to walk with you over here and show you something. Want to come along?

It's a beautiful sunny day in this place where we are together and we are strolling down a busy sidewalk. Let's take a right turn here and look in a few shop windows.

Come right along side me now. Look in this glass. Can you see yourself in the reflection? Don't look past your own face at the mannequins in their glamorous clothes. I want you to focus on yourself for just a minute.

What do you see?

I see someone real—someone beautiful and interesting, someone who has already accomplished a lot in life.

I'd like you to focus only on the best things in this mirror. Take a few minutes right now and write down what you see...

MY BEST STUFF

List your Top Ten Accomplishments in life so far on a new page of your notebook or journal.

"I have done...

See? We so often focus on our wounds and scars (which is normal because what hurts sticks out more than what doesn't) that we forget how amazing we really are. Don't worry if your accomplishments aren't grand or impressive compared to your friends, family, or what you see on television. In fact, that's part of the problem—comparison. I invite you to focus on those things which

FEEL important to you, whether they are large or small in the eyes of the world.

Before You Go To Sleep...

No matter how today went,
there's a very good chance you did the best you could.
And so, be extraordinarily gentle with yourself
as you fall asleep;
you want to be rested
and ready for the new day ahead.

DAY FIVE

If you knew that your passions and dreams
were gifts to motivate and lead you,
would you be more willing to take the next step?
Trust me; they are.

Following your passions and your dreams
is the greatest gift you could give the world.

Today I want to go back and talk about dreams again. I hope you can feel what is happening as we take this day-by-day walk together. You may not be noticing a lot of outward changes in your life yet, but the process of self-discovery and inner work is already well underway. Are you allowing each lesson or exercise to sink in and then start to sprout and grow roots throughout the day? I invite you to do that intentionally. Make a note to yourself to let your awareness return to the thought pattern for the day. When you set an intention to focus your mind like this, you will be surprised how many things appear to answer, in the most perfect ways, the questions or desires you have. It might be helpful to write down the main idea of each day on a note card or send yourself a text message—some way to keep the lesson at the top of your mind during the day.

In fact, the really cool thing is that you don't have to believe that these exercises will work—you only have to do them.

Today I'd like to show you the power you have to create "anchor points" using your mind. Sometimes if we have been going through a rough patch for a long time, it might seem like it will never end. I want to give you this method of recapturing a happy, resourceful state so you can begin to use that great energy to make changes in your current experience of life.

DREAMING AWAKE

Today I want to ask you to dream backward over the timeline of your life. Let your memory float until you find a time—an event or experience—when you felt *happy*. It's perfectly fine if you don't feel happy about anything in your life right now. Just locate one moment in your past when you FELT happy.

Do you have it yet?

Now I want you to make note of the feelings—not the details of the event so much, such as your age, the people involved, etc. Some of those things may be hard to duplicate in this experience. Instead please note the feelings in your body which you can remember with your physical senses.

Was the air warm or cold?

Were you inside a room or somewhere outside.

Was the light bright or dim?

Can you hear sounds like wind, music, voices?

Can you taste anything?

What do you smell?

How did your body feel?

Once you have accessed the memory fully, you will know it because you will _feel_ happy. If you keep having a wrestling match with your mind which tells you "...that was then. It's not true now", that's pretty normal. This just means you haven't let go all the way and gone back to that moment when you were in the state of happiness. Don't worry, this isn't a test and you won't fail if you can't get there with the first few tries.

Today I ask you to take a couple of short breaks and practice this. Go sit in your car or a quiet corner if necessary. When you can feel the moment from your memory all the way, just sit in it and experience everything.

You might wonder why I am asking you to do this. Do you feel a little silly about it or think that it isn't worth much in your life as it is today? If so, that's no problem.

What we are doing with this is exercising our mental and imaginative powers. We are directing the mind to do something it doesn't habitually do.

Now if you can go there and feel it all the way even once, you have done a big thing. You have changed your mental, emotional and physical state. You have that much power!

As we go along, I'll show you how to use this technology to begin taking steps toward much more of what you really want in your life. By the way, "happy" is just one state. If you are a real overachiever, play with other states like "powerful", "smart", "focused", "determined", or "brave".

BEFORE YOU GO TO SLEEP...

Do you remember the last time you were
content, at peace, relaxed, safe and calm?
Where were you?
Can you remember
the smells, the colors, the sounds
and who you were with?
Tonight when you get into bed,
paint the picture of that memory in your mind,
hug your pillow
and fall asleep with a smile.

PAUL S. BOYNTON

DAY SIX

Many of us want to do so many things
that we actually get stuck
because we can't choose which path to go down.
When you don't know what direction to move in –
just choose one –
give it a try;
see how you feel and what happens
and then re-assess and keep moving!
The only real way to discover your path
is one step at a time.

We have been dealing with some self-discovery work for the last few days. If you are anything like me, there are times when something inside just says, "Okay, I need to keep it real. How does this apply to my every day life?"

Well today I want to show you how to do exactly that.

In fact, I'm not going to talk a lot right now. I'll just give you something simple to do and then leave you to it. This will help us as we continue down the Begin With Yes road together.

WHAT I REALLY WANT IS...

Start a new page in your notebook. Draw a line down the middle. At the top of one column write **"More"** and at the top of the other write **"Less"**. Underneath those headings begin making a list (as quickly as you can—don't overthink this) of the things you want to fill your life and the things you want to leave your life.

I encourage you to be as specific as possible. It's okay to list feelings or ideas, but don't be afraid to write what is actually going on or specifically what you need and want.

Oh, also, please don't be afraid to write down something that someone else in your life might not like. This exercise isn't for your mother, your children, your partner, your boss, or anyone other than yourself.

"More of this... Less of this...

How did that go for you? I'm curious, is one side of the page longer than the other? Some of my friends find it much easier to identify what they don't want than what they do want in their lives. Others have been avoiding a good, close look at some unpleasant situations and it takes awhile to feel safe enough to really go there.

I invite you to be with this throughout the day. Add things as they come up in your mind. Now that you are placing clear focus on this, you will find that some things will come out of hiding and show themselves. As I instructed earlier, please keep this journal private. Your own honest thoughts, feelings and desires are so important and no one else needs to see what you have written.

BEFORE YOU GO TO SLEEP...

You know so much more then you may think.
You just need to find a quiet place to listen.
Maybe tonight just before you fall asleep
your heart will talk
and your mind will listen!

DAY SEVEN

The sooner I can shift into action,
the better off things become
and the sooner I begin to feel better.

Hello again!

Isn't it interesting how complicated we make things sometimes? Basically, we just want to FEEL good. In our work, in our bodies, in our relationships, in our social life—we want to feel good and not feel bad.

Consider how much complexity we layer on top of that simple desire. This reminds me of the quote from Fight Club, *"We buy things we don't need with money we don't have to impress people we don't like."* It's not just buying things either. Much of what we do in our lives is wasted energy that is spent chasing approval or acceptance from others while we pay almost no attention to what we really desire.

So today I want to offer you a simple way to begin doing something. *Begin With Yes* is a process. The process is a series of questions followed by subsequent manageable steps or actions, then more questions and actions, and so on.

We have been using this process in various ways for one week. Now I want you to experience what it is to use an answer to one of those questions and take a small but tangible step in your real life.

BABY STEPS...

Look at your lists from yesterday. Select just one item from either column, but only one. Write it at the top of a new page, then ask yourself, "what one small (maybe tiny) thing can I do today which will move me toward more of _____ or less of _____ ?"

Write down five to ten possible things you can actually do today. Let your mind go into its problem solving mode and offer you different approaches.

After you have several possibilities down on paper, please pick just one of them which you can and _will_ accomplish today. Just one really easy thing.

This might be as simple as getting on Craigslist and searching for possible new jobs, or going outside for a walk if you desire to improve your health.

"Just one small step today...

Now that you have that one "ridiculously easy" action item on paper, please raise your right hand and make a promise to yourself that you will do it today. If you have picked something which just doesn't fit into your schedule or requires much more courage than you feel right now, I ask you to go back and select one you know you can do.

BEFORE YOU GO TO SLEEP...

When you feel yourself
tensing up, pulling back and feeling scared;
remember you have gifts to be shared
and whisper, "yes."
Then breathe, smile and whisper "yes" again.
Repeat until you feel
the pit in your stomach releasing the tension.
And then fall asleep lighter and with a gentle smile.

Day Eight

*If you take one small step
toward resolving a challenge
or achieving a goal today,
you'll be that much further along
when you get into bed tonight.*

Yesterday we did a small stretching exercise. It's kind of like going to the gym or yoga class and loosening up before getting into the more vigorous work.

Today I want to expand upon what we did yesterday and apply it to bigger things in your life. Are you ready for that?

This is where it starts to get fun because now we are stepping forward in front of the canvas of the rest of our lives, picking up the paintbrush and beginning to paint a new picture.

Yesterday you selected just one thing from your "more of this... less of this" list and practiced directing your mind to come up with a tiny step.

Today we are going to push the gas pedal and move that into a higher gear.

PAINT YOUR PICTURE

Start a new journal page. As quickly as you can, write five dreams, goals or desires down. Leave several lines between each one. Underneath these headings, write small steps you could take *toward* them. These can be what at first appear to be too tiny or too easy. It doesn't even matter. Just let your creative mind take control and write down the steps you know you can take in the short term which will show that you are moving toward what you desire.

"I want this, and I could do this about it...

By the way, I'm not asking you to take these actions today. What we are doing here is reconditioning your mind to see the world of possibilities and potential. This is how you "begin with yes" in the real world.

Once you have your eyes open, don't be surprised when you get inspirations while you are taking a shower or driving or talking with a friend. That's how this works. You switch on your Possibility Radar when you allow yourself to imagine what you want and the simple, real-world steps you can take toward it.

See pages 30 - 33 of Begin With Yes for more on this.

BEFORE YOU GO TO SLEEP...

This could be the night
that you decide your dreams count
and you're ready to begin making them happen.
And if you decide that tonight is that night,
it will become one of those pivotal, magical
and beautifully stunning turning points
you'll remember with a grin
for the rest of your life.

DAY NINE

*The goal is not to avoid the fears
associated with an adventurous life.
The goal is to be so busy living a good one,
you hardly notice them.*

Today I would like to slow down just a little. Sometimes I have noticed that when I get into helping someone connect with possibilities, it's easy to get excited. I will watch them raise their vibration with me and begin to open themselves to new possibilities. I have often seen them pause like a cold breeze just touched the back of their neck. Their eyes get private and distant. When this happens, I know that they have internally retreated from something.

Do you know what that something is? Usually it is the unacknowledged fears and doubts which have stymied them in the past. Usually they are retreating from the journey into possibility because their mind is serving up old images of pain and failure. Their mind is saying, "Don't trust these new, positive feelings. All of this is too good to be true. You and I both know better."

So today I would like to take a few minutes and ask you to give those fears or doubts their voice. Does this sound strange coming from me—*Begin With Yes's* Optimist In Chief? Does it surprise you that I would actually encourage you to look at the negative? Being positive and bringing what you truly desire into your life is not about avoiding reality. In fact, this is the only way we help your mind trust this process. Once your mind knows that you will be honest—that you do have the courage to listen to its old stories—then it will relax and listen to the new stories you are telling it now.

FEAR, DOUBT & WORRY

On a new page of your notebook, write down the first 5-8 things you fear or doubt about some of the big new dreams you have painted for your future. You can write these in single words or short sentences. If you find that you have more to say underneath one of them, please do. Just be honest and let your mind chatter about why it believes that what you dream about and desire might not be possible.

"I'm not sure about this because...

How did that feel? Many people I work with have

reported that it felt like opening a valve and relieving a lot of pressure. Some of them have laughed and told me that they were completely surprised that I would let them say one negative thing. They were afraid that they were going to have to keep all those secret fears and worries corked up inside.

Well, this is how we deal with that pressure. We let it out. Now that it is outside of you, you have cleared space so what you truly wish to create can grow. It's like pulling weeds in your garden.

Before You Go To Sleep...

Sometimes I'm scared and anxious
and worry about things I can't control.
I make mistakes, have regrets, don't always get it right
and things don't always go my way.
Sure, I'll keep talking about dreams and goals
and small steps and hopefulness.
But please know I understand real life, real challenges
and difficult days and nights.
I understand because I walk that walk too.
And I believe that's what makes Begin with Yes
all the more powerful.
Things may not always happen easily
but when we really show up,
things always do begin to happen!

Day Ten

We can focus on what we can't do or what we can.
One slams the door shut; the other throws it wide open.

When you say YES to your life, you are actually
contributing to a universal YES that will impact others
in positive ways too. With that in mind, thanks for your
hopeful and inspiring energy!
And now, why not open your arms and hearts
to receive a little YES energy that your fellow travelers
have set in motion for you.

Good morning.

Notice the sun rising over there across the water? I
wanted to meet you here by the ocean again because I

want you to sit with me and listen to the sound these waves make for a few minutes.

Can you hear them now?

I'd like you to imagine that each wave which rolls in and washes across the sand toward us is saying "yes".

Over and over again, day and night since time began and even before that, nothing but "yes...yes...yes...yes...yes..."

Nature teaches us so much. It only knows "yes". Yes to the wind. Yes to the rain. Yes to sunshine, to earthquakes, to forest fires, to new Spring growth, to Summer heat. Yes to dropping leaves in the Fall. Yes to snow that drifts in great heaps during Winter.

We say "no" a lot. I'm not suggesting that we should never say no, but sometimes we get in such a habit of closing doors that we forget how to open them. When we remind ourselves how to say and feel "Yes", many new things can enter our lives—new possibilities, new opportunities, new strength and energy, and so much more.

The "No" Counter

Today I invite you to use your awareness to simply notice how many times you say or feel "no".

Each time you say or feel a "no" today,
don't correct yourself.
Just ask yourself what might be different
in the situation if you said "yes"
or opened yourself to the experience
in a new way.

This is not a writing exercise,
but if you get a big AHA,
please feel free to record it
and pay attention to how it unpacks
in your awareness.

If you want to make this an interesting game,
each time you get to "no"
make a mark on a sticky note or your hand.
At the end of the day count the marks.
The results will surprise you!

This reminds me of how we are taught to keep a food journal when we get into a weight loss program. The main value of this practice is to bring awareness to what we so often do unconsciously.

Yes and No each have their unique energy. When we learn how to shift into the energy of Yes more often, it is surprising how life responds by becoming much more expansive and fertile to help our desires and ideas take root.

BEFORE YOU GO TO SLEEP...

When we focus on all the things we don't have,
we miss the opportunity to appreciate,
be grateful for and enjoy all that we do have.
Tonight as you get ready for sleep,
focus on the "do haves."

DAY ELEVEN

If you know what you want,
then you're one step closer to it.
If you take a step in that direction
then you're actually making it happen.
Think small when it comes to steps
and big when it comes to dreams.

After someone who has read *Begin With Yes* makes a list of their dreams and goals, they often send me an email and say something like, *"...I'm so excited right now! Should I take my list and work on just one thing at a time before moving on to the next goal?"*

Although sometimes this is best, more often I advise them that working on many things at once can really raise the energy level and increase momentum across the board. I'm not talking about biting off way more than you can chew, but I am suggesting that you can begin taking lots of little steps toward at least several of these items on your Dream List.

When you are multi-tasking like this, it can be helpful to use a notebook to track the progress of your various ventures.

You may want to start a new notebook—nothing more elaborate than a legal pad is necessary. This one may well be something you use for years to come as you achieve great things and add more to your list.

GOAL PROGRESS NOTEBOOK

On a new page of your notebook write a goal at the top of the page. Underneath that list your first action step. Skip a few pages to leave room for more action steps, then do the process again for your next goal, and so on.

"My goal is _____

If you want to refer to *Begin With Yes*, the book, I explain this in more detail on pages 35 - 39.

Remember, I suggest not trying to come up with all the steps toward a goal in advance. Write the goal, come up with your first (extremely do-able) step, then do that. Once you have accomplished that step, write down the next one, and so on. It really is surprisingly simple when you approach anything this way, and it helps you stay out of the paralysis of analysis, too.

BEFORE YOU GO TO SLEEP...

Tonight,

imagine a warm, pure light surrounding you

and keeping you safe and soothed.

Rest gently knowing that as you sleep,

your mind, heart and soul

are conspiring to move you forward

in beautiful and wondrous ways

that will exceed anything you could possibly imagine.

Welcome it in.

DAY TWELVE

If you took one very small step today
towards something you've been dreaming about,
and then followed that step
each day this week with another . . . before you know it,
you'd no longer be dreaming,
you'd be doing!

Today as we meet I'm pretty sure I can read your mind. You seem to be thinking a lot of possibility thoughts, which makes me very happy. I also notice a few doubt clouds drifting around in your mind. You are wondering whether you can actually take on some of the big dreams you have had the courage to write down.

I'm not really a mind reader, of course, but I have worked

with my own *Begin With Yes* journey and that of so many other friends that it is a common thing at this stage to experience lingering anxiety.

There's good news here. You can accomplish your goals. If they are as magnificent as you are, though, you will need big resources to make them happen.

Today is about brainstorming to discover resources you have (or can acquire) to help you in your worthy quests. This is meant to be fun and invigorating.

BRAINSTORM

At the top of a new page, write one of your main goals. Underneath that start writing things you will need to accomplish it. Don't worry about staying inside the lines. Write quickly. Will you need money, people, technology, equipment, access, connections, mentors, or something else? Write it all down as fast as you can. Leave a little space around each one and let your mind serve up resources or connections you already have. Don't judge or eliminate them at this point. Just allow your mind to do what it does best—plan, identify, and make associations between things.

"I will need _____

I often watch people have major breakthroughs at this stage. Where before they could only see how limited they are, after they have laid the foundation of writing down their goals, first steps, and then writing out all the needed resources, it is surprising how quickly they see just how much is at their disposal to accomplish their dreams. In fact, just the process of detailing what they will need usually helps them gain amazing clarity on other action steps.

Please get this started and then let your mind work on it in the background today as you go about your other business. Once you give your mind a job like this, it loves to please you. Remember, you are the boss of your mind and you can give it whatever tasks you wish. When you think of more things you will need, just jot them down on this page. If you start to feel overwhelmed, take a break. This exercise is meant to inspire you, not stress you out. You will begin to acquire these resources in the *Begin With Yes* way—one step at a time.

I should also remind you that when you focus your energy and attention in this way, you activate the mysterious forces of the Universe to rally in your favor. I won't try to explain this, but once you have mustered the courage to clarify what you want and what you need, things start to show up in the most extraordinary ways to support exactly that. I want you to experience this for yourself.

Before You Go To Sleep...

What your heart yearns for is not just a desire,
it's a calling!
Don't just listen, answer.

The last things we think about and talk about
before we fall asleep,
stay with us as we sleep.
So choose wisely dear friends.

PAUL S. BOYNTON

DAY THIRTEEN

You do not have to move mountains today.
Start with a small rock or two and repeat.
Stay focused on the small stones
and the mountain moving will take care of itself!

You know how we sometimes meet like this and sit on a bench watching the sun rise or sip coffee together in a snug little espresso shop?

Well today is something different. Let's take a brisk walk starting right now. Are you ready to go?

As we walk, taking long strides and breathing deep, feel the energy rising up through your body. What we are doing is flipping our power switch to the "on" position. This is where we move all this *Begin With Yes* energy from the mental and emotional zone into physical action.

Many people ask me how they can dip into the deep well of their plans, hopes, dreams and fears and draw out the raw power they need to move forward. It's easy to get stuck sometimes, isn't it?

Today I want to help you use some of that energy you have been plugging into over the last twelve days. You have already done the inner work, now it's time to push the "on" button.

Go Time!

Don't write anything down today until _after_ you have taken one simple action step.

Select just one of the goals from your Goal Progress Notebook (we talked about this on Day 12). Find the action step you wrote down. Then do it.

<u>After</u> you have completed that one thing, please write it down in your daily notebook.

"I did this _____ today...

Most likely by now you will also already know what the next natural step after that should be and I recommend that you write that under its goal in your Goal Progress Notebook.

Can you feel how powerful this is?

You just took a step toward a goal or dream which has lived dormant inside you. Now you are moving and your mind is activated.

You may find that you have built up a head of steam and have energy to accomplish some of the other "first action steps" under some of your other goals. If this is true, don't hesitate to do those, too!

If you need a refresher on this information, you can find the Power Switch section starting on page 60 of *Begin With Yes*.

Before You Go To Sleep…

Waiting for our lives to begin or restart or take off
is a trick of the mind that keeps us stuck.
Deciding that we're not going to wait another moment
and taking one small step into the unknown
is our soul declaring, "I have begun."
Think of one small action you can take tonight
that will set you up to take another small step tomorrow
and your wait will be over!

Day Fourteen

Things,
especially life-changing important things,
are often hard
but seldom impossible!

Today is a good day. Will you imagine that we are standing together in a lush green forest? The air is cool and the sun is filtering through the branches of the tall fir trees all around us. Let's just stretch and feel the light enter our bodies and minds for a few minutes.

Every journey needs some stretches of downhill path so we can catch our breath and take a look back to see how far we've come.

For today I prescribe a little looking back. You have made real progress and I want to be sure you both see and feel it. This is also a chance to be honest about areas that don't feel so great or where you may have stumbled here and there.

Imagine that you have been on a long uphill hike and you have come to a soft green meadow with a stream running through it which just invites you to sit and rest. You take your boots off, strip off your socks and dip your sore toes in the water. Notice how high you have climbed already and also the places on you that might have some scrapes or bumps from the trail. This is a good spot to do some self care and get ready for the rest of your trip to the summit.

Reality Check

Take a few minutes and glance back over your notes from the beginning. Try to remember your state of mind and how you were feeling about life when you started. Do you notice a difference between then and now? Do you have any "bumps or scrapes" which need attention? Write a paragraph or two about this in your notebook.

"My notes from the road...

After you write down a few of your feelings about the road thus far, I encourage you to do something nice for yourself. Maybe get a massage or your favorite beverage.

Take some time to rest yourself mentally, emotionally and physically. You are doing great work and your focus, energy, and determination are getting stronger right before our eyes.

Before You Go To Sleep...

The first step is so important,
but it's only with the second step
that we fully let go of where we were
and that's when our next adventure
officially begins.
Sending you hope, courage and love tonight
as you step into the beautiful space of becoming!

DAY FIFTEEN

There is no one more important
or less important than you.
Your dreams count just as much as those of anyone else.
And the way to realize your dreams
is the same way everyone realizes dreams: Action!
I plan to make today count and hope you do too.

I hope yesterday was full of rest and healing for you. Today I would like to pick up where we left off by asking you to select one or two of those "bumps or scrapes"— things you have tried since you started this *Begin With Yes* journey which haven't quite worked out as planned.

If you were learning to play guitar or tennis, you would

experience many off notes or missed serves. That's just part of the process and no one would look down on you for that. It's expected!

The trouble is that we often get critical and beat ourselves up when it comes to our attempts at small steps toward what's closest to our hearts—our hopes, dreams and goals.

Today, rather than writing anything down, I invite you to pick out one or two missteps which left you feeling quietly discouraged and find a way to either do them again (like practicing your tennis serve after missing one) or perhaps try a different approach.

Will you do that?

This is part of the honest, courageous process of becoming what is possible. Rather than painting a brave face over these things, it is much better to look at them, acknowledge what hurts, then take another step in the right direction.

If you want to take one or two new steps and then write

about it in your notebook, that would be great. I'm confident that you will experience fresh confidence by doing this.

Before You Go To Sleep...

If you haven't been rejected, you haven't lived!
We're all bound to get rejection letters,
broken hearts and "no thanks" phone calls.
There'll always be someone who won't like
our website, our book, our resume, our work, the way
we dress, laugh, or tie our shoes
(and they'll be happy to tell us, too).
We can dwell on the rejection,
or we can seek out people who lift us up
and then take a deep breath
and shift our attention to moving forward with
our days, our evenings and our lives.

PAUL S. BOYNTON

DAY SIXTEEN

We've been taught that sticks and stones
may break our bones, and words will never hurt us.
But that's not true.
Words can be incredibly powerful,
especially the words we use when talking to ourselves.
Begin to carefully listen;
what are you telling yourself
about your dreams, your goals, your hopes
and the challenges you face?
And as you listen, ask yourself if you need a re-write
that is more positive, hopeful and encouraging.

Change is in the air. Can you feel it?

Today I would like you to notice how things are shifting in your life. In *Begin With Yes* I talked about how you don't have to start out as a positive, enthusiastic person to have these principles work. I'm curious, though. Have you noticed that you have become more open to new possibilities and automatically look for synchronicity as it appears to support your decisions and actions?

If so, this means you are growing. No, you are not changing into someone you're not or putting on a false front. You are simply expanding into more of the dynamic creature you are.

"Self talk" is very important right now. Noticing how you speak to yourself and about yourself is one way you can revise the old picture of your life. As the Persian poet Hafiz once said, *"The words you speak become the house you dwell in."*

I would be remiss if I didn't also point out that it is important to notice those people in your life who support you—and those who don't. Now that your growth is showing up in the real world, you will find that some people are your cheerleaders, always looking for ways to encourage you, while others seem to want to add weight to your life.

The people I speak to about this often ask me how to handle those situations when people are negative or resistant to the changes they are making.

In pages 69-74 of *Begin With Yes*, I shared some thoughts on this important topic. It may be a good time to read that short section again for reflection.

THE PEOPLE LEDGER

Start a new page in your notebook and draw a line down the middle. At the top of one column draw a "+ " and on the other a "— ". Begin to think about those people who are part of your every day life: family members, friends, business associates, and social contacts. As each face appears in your mind, feel whether your current relationship with them is light or heavy, "plus or minus". Without overthinking it, write their name in one column or the other.

"Is this relationship light or heavy in my life...

PAUL S. BOYNTON

I encourage you to keep this page strictly private, just like the rest of this notebook. This isn't a matter of judging these people or immediately cutting them out of your life. All you are doing right now is identifying relationships with people and how they affect you as you shift into a new way of being.

By being honest about how each relationship currently feels, you are simply acknowledging this snapshot in time. As I say in *Begin With Yes*, when you continue toward your inspired vision for your life, some people will naturally move away from you. You may need to draw some clear, firm boundaries with others. For today, all I ask is that you shine the light on where things stand. Who is a supporter and who is a detractor?

With this awareness, in the days ahead you will naturally begin to be more alert, be clear, set some boundaries, avoid trying to control others, and remind yourself that your new approach is just plain better for you and the world.

BEFORE YOU GO TO SLEEP...

Tonight, find a quiet place to be alone for a few minutes
and just practice breathing.
With each breath,
imagine your body relaxing and your heart opening.
Trust that at this moment,
you are here on purpose
and things are unfolding
the way they were meant to unfold.
And as you get ready to sleep tonight,
invite in thoughts of hope, enthusiasm
and a vision for the days ahead.
And rest easy; you deserve it.

PAUL S. BOYNTON

Day Seventeen

*It's essential to have people in our life
to encourage and to remind us of our potential
in a hopeful, optimistic and empowering way.
We attract those people by being one of them.*

It's time we talk about this idea of mentors and guides. I'll never forget when I read this quote from Albert Schweitzer, *"In everyone's life, at some time, our inner fire goes out. It is then burst into flame by an encounter with another human being. We should all be thankful for those people who rekindle the inner spirit."* I'm not sure about you, but I have had many of those people in my life and I can never fully say "thank you" for what they have meant to me.

Our twenty-one day journey is rapidly coming to a close, but that means that your *Begin With Yes* lifestyle is just getting started. At this point it will be good to identify some people who can help you stay on track as you bring your dreams and goals into reality.

You may be surprised by exactly who these people are and how they show up in your life. One thing I know for sure is that they will appear and their help will come at critical moments. You may already know them or they may be waiting in the wings for the right moment.

My Mentors

It is entirely possible that your mentors are already in your life. You may just need to ask for their wisdom and guidance.

It will help if you can review your goals or dreams and identify specific areas in which you know for sure you will need advice beyond your current level of experience. If someone comes immediately to your mind, note them as a possible mentor. For now just get clear on what aspects of your goals require expert knowledge. This exercise will activate the part of your mind which will begin seeking exactly the right people and be able to recognize them when they appear.

"I need guidance in these areas...

Wisdom comes in many forms. Sometimes it will manifest as a person with knowledge to share, but it may also show up in a book, a movie, or some synchronistic circumstance of your life—it might even happen on a Facebook page with people you've never met in person before.

Right now you are turning on your antennae to receive the signals in whatever ways they find their way to you. I predict that you will begin noticing all kinds of information and resources—and that the best possible mentors will begin presenting themselves precisely when you need them. I encourage you to pay better attention than usual because sometimes they show up in funny disguises. Often they are hiding in plain sight!

PAUL S. BOYNTON

Before You Go To Sleep...

There are things that we already know
that we haven't yet allowed ourselves to fully see.
Maybe it's a change we need to make,
a relationship that needs to shift,
a goal we need to focus on,
or a dream that needs to be put front and center.
Simply asking yourself the question,
"What do I know that I haven't let myself see?"
is one good way to discover deep truths
that can change your life
in profound and wonderful ways.

Day Eighteen

We are like a magnificent tree: expansive and deep.
Our branches and leaves grow towards the light—
evolving, reaching, unfolding and becoming.
And our deep roots ground us, holding us steady
connecting us in solid, reliable and reassuring ways.
We may forget this
but forgetting never changes who we are.

When we take small, consistent steps towards
what "could be", we are actually joining force
with the Universe to co-create what "will be."

Sometimes when we decide to focus on transformation for a period of time, it is easy to forget that we are always in the process of becoming. Today I invite you to spend some time appreciating how far you have already come. Did you know many experts say that twenty-one days is the length of time it takes to establish a new habit? This workbook is set up with twenty-one days on purpose to help you create a foundation for this *Begin With Yes* way of life.

By now you may have noticed some measurable progress. It's likely that you have already taken steps which made visible impact in your career, family life, social circles, or other areas. It is also possible that what you see most is a marked difference in your state of mind. Do you find yourself approaching the challenges and frustrations of daily life with a new sense of personal power?

I would like you to take a little time to mark your progress. This is an important part of what is known as "positive feedback loops". Whenever we move in a new, positive direction, if we get reinforcement that our choices are working, it bolsters our determination to keep going. For example, if you have ever lost significant weight and people start saying, "You look great! I almost didn't recognize you", doesn't that help you stay focused on all those behaviors which helped you drop the pounds?

Progress Notes

Start a new page in your notebook. Look back to the time when you started this work and notice anything which tells you that you are making progress. Write a few sentences describing what those things are and how you feel about them.

"I see visible change in these areas...

We are often our own harshest critics. Many of us had parents, teachers or other authority figures who pointed out the flaws in our behavior, and we got in the habit of following their example by looking for what we haven't done well. This is an opportunity to erase some of those old tapes running in the background of your mind. Get used to paying attention to what you are doing right and appreciating yourself for the real progress you are making.

Before You Go To Sleep...

If we aren't willing to look beyond
our current situations,
we will miss incredible opportunities
to create new realities!
And just because it can sometimes be
a challenge to do that – doesn't mean we can't.
Tonight focus on the possibilities
and get some good rest!

PAUL S. BOYNTON

DAY NINETEEN

It's kind of funny,
we tend to think of small steps
as really not all that effective,
and we use that as an excuse to stand still.
When in reality it's those small steps
that make most of those big changes happen.

Today I want to address something which just can't be left out of a practical, honest approach to moving ahead in life.

On pages 75-76 in *Begin With Yes*, I address the fact that this process is not therapy. It is a deliberate, on point, action-based redirection in response to challenges and opportunities. In my work with people, I sometimes need to point them in the direction of a therapist or other professional. Often they have been struggling with big issues and were afraid that it would be somehow admitting weakness if they got help from one of these qualified experts. Isn't that interesting? We aren't squeamish about going to the doctor when we are sick or to a dentist if we have a toothache, but when the pain exists in our minds or emotions, we often feel that we must just keep soldiering along and hope it gets better.

As I wrote in *Begin With Yes*, "A depressed person can still be a *Begin With Yes* person by acknowledging the pain and asking, 'What do I need to do to get to a better place?' The answer might very well be to find a good therapist and begin therapy. That moment of awareness followed by action (scheduling an appointment and beginning a therapeutic process) will be a major 'yes' step moving the person in a more hopeful direction."

Begin With Yes is a process designed to get you moving— no matter where you start, or what obstacle you need to work through.

Today I invite you to reflect on your life path. Now that

you have been doing this intentional self-discovery work, you are going to be better at spotting patterns. If you notice, for example, that you have great ideas but find yourself getting depressed shortly after you start a new project, throw up your hands and say, "What's the use? I can't sustain the energy I'll need to get this done...", it could be that a professional could help you get to the root cause very quickly.

I won't prescribe a specific writing assignment today, but if you start to identify an "elephant in the room", it might help to write it down in your notebook and consider the most simple, direct way of addressing it.

The truth is, there are some breakthroughs for which we need the help of others who are qualified to advise us and offer real tools. I know this has been the case in my life and I have seen some amazing shifts in the lives of people who have read my book after they take steps like this, too.

Do you have any "hiding in plain sight" obstacles coming up for you? Let today be one when you open yourself and allow those answers to surface. As they do, please be gentle with yourself. As one of my dear friends sometimes says, "Things only come up for us when we're strong enough to handle them." If these are old, chronic problems for you, the fact that you are willing to let them come up now means you are getting stronger. You are making progress!

BEFORE YOU GO TO SLEEP...

Resting deeply requires us to
temporarily surrender
the worries, the dreams, the fears,
the plans and the circular thinking
that tends to preoccupy our waking moments.
And resting deeply is so important
because it allows break-through shifts in perspective
that will open new doorways
that can change everything for the better.

DAY TWENTY

Today,
why not find someone
who has less than you
and share a little of what you have.

Yesterday I used the phrase "elephant in the room" and I think it is time to look at a big one. Don't worry, this won't be hard.

The word is Happiness. We all want that, don't we?

When people are buried in problems and lost in tangles of painful circumstances, they often feel that happiness is something they just missed when they were in the line where Happy Genes were being passed out. Even when they get involved with *Begin With Yes*, it is easy to assume that the most important thing is to plug along with small action steps and hope that life improves over time. The journey seems so long at times, doesn't it?

Well, today I want to come right out and say it. At its core, *Begin With Yes* is all about living a happy life. I have found that living a life full of honesty, courage, commitment to our highest values, and taking action toward our true desires sets our sails in the direction of happiness no matter which way the wind is blowing at the moment. Some other words which come to mind are Purpose, Meaning, Freedom, and Achievement.

Those are big, powerful words, but I want to bring this down to ground level. One of the quickest ways to feel happy is to spread small seeds happiness around you. I'm sure you are familiar with the idea of "random acts of kindness". Today I invite you to scheme up several little things you can do on purpose to bring more happiness into the world around you.

Plotting Happiness

Take just a few minutes in your notebook and come up with three to five small things you will do today to surprise and delight people in your life. It might be fun to do something for total strangers. If you need some ideas, go to page 101 in Begin With Happiness. I know you and your creative nature will come up with even more on your own, too.

"I will sprinkle happiness seeds today..."

As fun and easy as this might sound, I am not just being whimsical by inviting you to spread happiness. These are "yes" steps which are proven to alter our own moods, brighten the energetic sphere of our lives, and set other good things in motion. Please don't believe me—try it for yourself.

When we become part of the solution in this way, we truly change the world. Yes, these are small things and they aren't hard to accomplish. They also help us get what eludes so many people all their lives—happiness.

I wish I could explain why this works in scientific terms. Since I can't, I just want to say that I know from my own experience that when I move in the direction of happiness by shifting into this state using small actions, I watch the world brighten up around me. Something surprising is activated which also helps me achieve my greater goals more easily.

Can you see how this is a core principle behind the entire *Begin With Yes* process?

Before You Go To Sleep...

It's kind of funny,
we tend to think of small steps
as really not all that effective,
and we use that as an excuse to stand still.
When in reality it's those small steps
that make most of those big changes happen.

DAY TWENTY ONE

There is absolutely no doubt
that a positive, hopeful attitude
combined with one-step-at-a-time actions
create powerful new realities.
And there's absolutely no doubt
that you have what it takes
to take at least one small step today.

Here we are at Day Twenty One. I have loved our times together. In some way I feel like we really have been walking and talking through this process. Today isn't about saying goodbye, though. This is a big "hello" to the rest of your life.

I do want to distill the *Begin With Yes* process again, though, so you can easily remember it whenever you find yourself feeling stuck or confused about what you should do next.

Basically, it comes down to answering these three questions:

- Where am I right now?
- Where do I want to go?
- What is the first possible step I can take in that direction?

I know that isn't a complicated formula, but I use it over and over again in my own life.

Since we have been talking about this as a journey, I'd like to remind you that when we get moving down the path of our goals and dreams, the landscape changes. We experience ups and downs. We find ourselves at the top of new mountains and feel like we can see forever. We walk through long, shadowy valleys and wonder if we will ever see sunshine again. Because this is true, we need a compass to help us stay on course.

Those three questions will act as a compass. They get our

feet back on the ground, get us pointed in the right direction, and help us have confidence about stepping forward again.

Today I'm asking you to take stock again. You have already changed in the last few weeks and the view from where you stand today probably looks different.

Let's establish this *Begin With Yes* habit even more deeply right now, shall we?

COMPASS QUESTIONS

Please start a new page in your notebook. Write down the three questions.

- Where am I right now?

- Where do I want to go?

- What is the first possible step I can take in that direction?

Now answer them based upon where you are today.

"Here's how things stand and where I'm going...

PAUL S. BOYNTON

You should know how much I respect you for making this commitment to yourself. Twenty-one days of focused self-discovery and action is no small accomplishment. By doing this, you have come to the front of the crowd. You may not know it yet, but you are a leader. You are one of the small (but rapidly growing) percentage of people who have made a clear decision to accept the responsibility for creating a life and a world which is happier, richer, kinder, and more beautiful. You can't help but raise the standard for what it means to be an excellent human when you do this.

So I want to take my hat off to you right now and say, "Thank you from the bottom of my heart."

Oh, and I know that you may be one of those people who just couldn't stop reading every day and maybe you didn't complete the daily exercises. Remember that this process is sort of like a spiral staircase. It goes around and around, each step takes us gradually higher as we circle the central lessons. Rather than close this book and look for the next positivity fix, I encourage you to go back to Day One and review this workbook again. If you did the exercises, maybe you can read over your notes and add to or revise them a bit. If you skipped any assignments, maybe you can go ahead and do them now. Either way, you will get the biggest benefit from this course of action by continuing the process over and over again. Each time we gain new ground, the landscape changes and so does the horizon. We see different things and bigger dreams. We face new fears and gain more clarity.

To really make these ideas become part of your life, I suggest that you write down the main lesson or assignment from each day on a note card or send yourself a text message—find some way to keep it at the top of your mind throughout your day. When you do this, you add extra awareness to situations which were previously unconscious. This creates a conscious "choice point" and you get to exercise your powers of free will and creativity to shape the situation from a fresh perspective.

As your own journey continues, please accept my love and gratitude. I have no doubt our paths will cross again at the perfect time and I can't wait to learn of your progress.

With anticipation,

Paul S. Boynton
Optimist In Chief
Begin With Yes

Begin With Yes: The 10 Principles

1. Begin - The best time to start is now.

2. Have a sense of hopefulness and roll up your sleeves.

3. Expect that Begin with Yes will train your mind to think in an open, creative way and empower your problem-solving capacity.

4. Remember, the secret to a good life is less about having a positive attitude and more about taking positive actions.

5. Ask questions. There are always answers to be found and the answers lead to actions that will move you forward.

6. Keep moving one step at a time. Don't let fear stop you.

7. Find your power by taking action.

8. Focus on finding people you can help, rather than on people to help you.

9. It's not one great big "yes." It's a thousand little "yeses" that make life-changing things happen.

10. Begin.

ABOUT THE AUTHOR

Paul Boynton *is the President & CEO of The Moore Center. He also blogs for The Huffington Post and The Good Men's Project, is a columnist for the NH Business Review and the host of "Begin with Yes" on Empower Radio. He is the author of several books including "Begin with Yes". His Facebook community, which has over a million followers is a source of inspiration for those who are taking steps toward a more meaningful life. You can read more at www.beginwithyes.com or on Facebook at www.Facebook.com/beginwithyes*

MORE BOOKS BY PAUL S. BOYNTON

Find these books and more by this author at Amazon.com

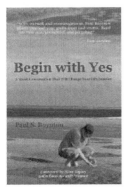 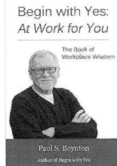 

Join Paul Boynton and over a million Begin With Yes friends from around the world on Facebook!

www.Facebook.com/BeginWithYes

Visit the author at his website and subscribe for email updates
& inspiring newsletters

www.BeginWithYes.com

If you love this book and want to help others find it, please take a moment and post a review on Amazon. Thank you!